D1716818

HAUNTED PLACES

BY JOHN HAMILTON

VISIT US AT
WWW.ABDOPUBLISHING.COM

Published by ABDO Publishing Company, 4940 Viking Drive, Suite 622, Edina, Minnesota 55435.
Copyright ©2007 by Abdo Consulting Group, Inc. International copyrights reserved in all countries.
No part of this book may be reproduced in any form without written permission from the publisher.
ABDO & Daughters™ is a trademark and logo of ABDO Publishing Company.

Printed in the United States.

Editor: Sue Hamilton
Graphic Design: Sue Hamilton
Cover Design: Neil Klinepier
Cover Illustration: *Death*, ©1977 Don Maitz
Interior Photos and Illustrations: p 1 *Maitz Motel,* ©1996 Don Maitz; p 4 Figure in spooky woods, Corbis; p 5 *Final Defender,* ©1981 Janny Wurts; pp 6-7 *Beneath an Opal Moon,* ©1981 Don Maitz; p 8 (top) Whaley House, courtesy San Diego Save Our Heritage Organization; (bottom) Borley Rectory, Mary Evans; p 9 Borley Rectory Ghosts, Mary Evans; p 10 (left) Cemetery sign, courtesy Forest Lawn Memorial Gardens Cemetery; (right) Rocky and Barbara Marciano, Corbis; p 11 Spooky graveyard, Corbis; pp 12-13 *Death,* ©1977 Don Maitz; p 15 *Curse of the Mistwraith,* ©1993 Janny Wurts; pp 16-17 *Mistwraith's Bane,* ©1992 Janny Wurts; p 18 Union and Confederate reenactors, AP Images; p 19 *Search Wraith,* ©1991 Janny Wurts; p 20 Gettysburg, AP Images; p 21 Reenactment of Antietam, AP Images; p 22 Queen Anne Hotel, iStockphoto; p 23 (top) *Maitz Motel,* ©1996 Don Maitz; (bottom) *Psycho,* courtesy Universal Pictures; p 24 *Haunted Hops,* ©1995 Don Maitz; p 25 Chumley's, AP Images; p 27 *Shipwrecker,* ©1982 Janny Wurts; p 28 Lighthouse in dark clouds, Corbis; p 29 Moon over Ludlow's Lighthouse, AP Images; p 31 *Desperation: The Well,* ©1995 Don Maitz.

Library of Congress Cataloging-in-Publication Data

Hamilton, John, 1959-
  Haunted places / John Hamilton.
     p. cm. -- (The world of horror)
  Includes index.
  ISBN-13: 978-1-59928-768-3
  ISBN-10: 1-59928-768-4
  1. Haunted places--Juvenile literature. I. Title.

BF1461.H294 2007
133.1'2--dc22

                                2006032743

CONTENTS

HAUNTED PLACES

Fog flows in eerie, snakelike trails across a silent cemetery and through the surrounding dark woods. Is it a natural phenomenon, or the restless soul of a ghost? The creaks and groans of an aging house can be heard even in daylight. Is it the sound of the building's wood expanding and contracting, or its dead owners unwilling to leave their earthly home?

Haunted places have existed for centuries. From fog-shrouded castles to misty battlegrounds to lonely lighthouses, ghosts of the past seem to linger in certain places.

South England's countryside is host to the mysterious place known as Stonehenge. Huge stones form a circular monument. Once used by the ancient Druids, priests of the British Isles' Celtic society, the area has become known as a place for ghosts and demons.

Forests, by their very nature, seem to hold mystery and danger. Tall trees block the sunlight, creating a place of darkness. For some people, the woods are places of muted beauty, while others see every tree trunk and shadowy brush as a hiding place for ghouls and spooks.

Churches, usually thought of as places of safety and comfort, also reportedly hold the spirits of those unable to rest in peace. Stories of religious leaders, often those who led a less-than-spiritual life, sometimes haunt the buildings in which they once preached.

From culture to culture, places exist that are home to everything from quiet ghosts to noisy poltergeists. Sometimes, a spirit just doesn't seem to want to leave its favorite place. More often, a certain past event is the source of the place's haunting. Violence and death yield stories of unfortunate souls who remain earthbound, haunting the rooms, halls, fields, trails, and burial grounds of the world.

Below: A spectral figure walks past a pond in a spooky forest.

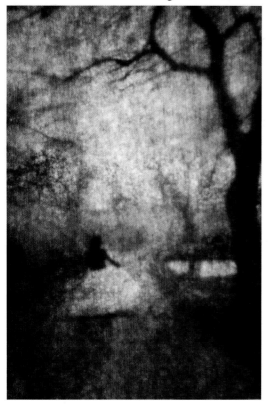

Above: Final Defender by Janny Wurts. An English wizard faces ghosts at Stonehenge.

Haunted Houses

The image most people have of a haunted house is a run-down, abandoned building with broken windows, creaky floors, and spiderwebs everywhere. However, in reality, ghostly activity is reported in new houses as well as old. Sometimes the homes are empty, but usually people live alongside the ghostly occupants.

The Whaley House

The Whaley House of San Diego, California, has the questionable distinction of being named the most haunted house in the United States. Two of the ghosts are the original owners, Thomas and Anna Whaley. Thomas has been seen standing on the house's upper landing. Anna Whaley drifts in and out of the garden, as well as the downstairs rooms. However, back in 1856, when the Whaleys first moved into the house, the family experienced their own haunting.

The earliest ghostly resident of Whaley House is "Yankee Jim." A few years before the house was built, the thief James Robinson was hanged on the very site. Although Thomas Whaley witnessed the 1852 hanging, four years later he bought the land and built his home there.

Right: Beneath an Opal Moon by Don Maitz.

Above: The Whaley House of San Diego, California, has been named the most haunted house in the United States.

After the family moved in, they began hearing heavy footsteps. They were convinced it was Yankee Jim Robinson, noisily stomping his way through their home. For decades, various members of the Whaley family continued to hear the footsteps.

Today the Whaley House is a historic museum. After-hours ghostly tours bring in the curious believers and nonbelievers. Other ghosts have occasionally been reported, including that of an unknown woman, a young child, and even the Whaley's terrier, Dolly Varden. This quiet California place, whose upper-level windows open by themselves, seems to be filled with ghosts.

The Borley Rectory

A ghostly nun already walked the land on which the Borley Rectory was built in 1863 for Rev. Henry Bull and his family. The villagers of Borley, England, had repeatedly seen the sorrowful figure of the woman strolling along "Nun's Walk." They believed she was a former nun who had fallen in love with a monk at the Borley Monastery. The two had tried to run off together, but were discovered. Supposedly, the wayward monk was executed, and the poor nun was walled up in the cellars of the monastery.

Right: The Borley Rectory, a home built in 1863 for use by the Borley Church's minister, Rev. Henry Bull, is believed to be the most haunted house in England.

Perhaps it was all a gruesome story, but the Bull family, as well as their servants and guests, began to see the lady peering at them through the windows and gliding across the lawn—even in daylight hours. The nun wasn't the only ghostly spirit. A phantom carriage and horses were also seen racing up the drive.

In 1927, Rev. Lionel Foyster and his family moved into the rectory. His young wife, Marianne, became the center of the ghosts' attention. Horrified witnesses saw messages to Marianne scrawled on the walls of the house. Most were unreadable, but one said, "Marianne, please help get." Rev. Foyster had the house exorcised in an attempt to drive out the spirits, but the haunting continued. The Foysters finally left, and no other ministers would live there.

Psychic researcher Harry Price began a year-long investigation of the house in 1937. Together with 48 volunteers, he recorded an incredible number of mysterious happenings. During a séance on March 27, 1938, a ghost warned that the rectory would burn down. Eleven months later, it did. Witnesses reported seeing ghostly figures amidst the flames and a nun's face peering out from an upper window.

However, even after the house was destroyed, and continuing to this day, the land where the rectory once stood, as well as the nearby Borley Church, still have reports of ghostly activities. Perhaps the ghosts have nowhere else to go?

Above: An illustration of the spirit nun and ghostly horse-drawn carriage, both of which were said to haunt the Borley Rectory.

SCARY CEMETERIES

Cemeteries seem like a natural place for ghostly activities. Hundreds of dead bodies lie silently in their final resting places. Creepy by nature, not all cemeteries have resident spooks, but a few graveyards host a number of active, sometimes bold, ghosts.

Boxing legend Rocky Marciano and his wife Barbara are buried at Forest Lawn Memorial Gardens in Fort Lauderdale, Florida. The ghostly couple are frequently seen by visitors who have come to see the heavyweight champion's grave.

The Marcianos aren't the only ghosts in this haunted cemetery. Many people report a barefoot man wearing a tie-dye shirt and bell-bottom pants. The ghost taps mourners on the shoulder and asks for a light for his cigarette. When someone turns around, the hippy-looking phantom vanishes.

Another ghost, named Diane, who dresses in a pink gown, frequently walks in front of approaching vehicles. The long-haired specter creepily disappears when a car drives over her.

This busy cemetery has repeatedly been visited by ghost hunters and paranormal investigators, but whether these spirits are real or imaginary remains an ongoing mystery.

Above: The front of the haunted Forest Lawn Memorial Gardens Cemetery.

Above: Barbara and Rocky Marciano, shortly after one of Rocky's fights.

Above: A spooky cemetery at dusk.

Death by
Don Maitz.

There are hundreds of cemeteries where ghostly activity occurs. Ghosts of all shapes and sizes—male, female, young and old—are found in graveyards throughout the world. It is believed that ghosts are the result of deadly, traumatic events. Spirits remain in the earthly realm because they have unfinished business that was cut short. They usually haunt the location of their death. However, since very few people actually die in cemeteries, how is it that so many specters appear in these locations?

Some people believe that these ghosts are tied to cemeteries because of events that happened *after* the spirits' deaths. Perhaps some items belonging to the dead people were stolen from them. Maybe they have no grave markers, or their burial places have been forgotten because their families have moved away. Whatever the case, these ghosts remain in the area where their physical remains are located, and reports of these graveyard ghosts are frequent and widespread.

CREEPY CASTLES

astles were built for war. With their thick, high walls, they were very hard to attack. Armies were based in these fortresses, and they were also the homes of kings and queens, knights and peasants, and lords and ladies. Most castles in Europe were built during the last half of the Middle Ages, between 1000 and 1450 A.D. Many were occupied for hundreds of years. Their stony walls witnessed much violence and intrigue, including wars, rebellions, murders, and torture. It's not surprising that most castles have at least one ghost story to tell.

Duntrune Castle

Below: Duntrune Castle. Mysterious bagpipe music can sometimes be heard echoing through the castle's halls.

Duntrune Castle was built in the 12th century. It is the oldest, continuously inhabited building in Scotland. Located on Loch Crinan, overlooking the Sound of Jura, it is also home to a ghost.

In the 1600s, an invading Irishman named Coll MacDonnell approached the castle, which at that time was home to the Campbells of Duntrune. Before attacking, MacDonnell sent his bagpiper forward to spy on the castle's defenses. The piper was captured and thrown into one of the castle's towers. Looking out the turret window, he saw his lord's ship approaching. He played a warning song from his bagpipe, which caused MacDonnell to turn his ship safely around.

Above: Curse of the Mistwraith by Janny Wurts. In Europe, many haunted castles still stand. Their stony walls were witness to everything from war and violence, to love and intrigue.

The angry Campbells immediately had the piper's hands cut off, and then butchered him. For many years afterward, even after the castle passed into the hands of the McCallum Clan, the ghostly sound of distant bagpipes echoed through the halls of Duntrune Castle. In 1910, workers found the fingerless skeleton of a man within the castle walls. And in the 1960s, while the castle kitchen was being renovated, workmen found two skeleton hands under the floor. Even though the skeleton was given a proper burial, the eerie bagpipe music can still occasionally be heard.

Dunrobin Castle

Scotland's Dunrobin Castle is said to be haunted by a specter. Witnesses claim it is the ghost of the daughter of the castle's 14th Earl, who had her imprisoned in the attic for her wicked ways. She tried to escape by climbing out a window, but instead fell to her death. Now her ghost roams the upper floors of the castle.

Above: Mistwraith's Bane by Janny Wurts.

The Tower of London

The Tower of London is home to many ghosts. Some say it's the most haunted castle in all of Europe. William the Conqueror, King of England, started construction of the fortress in the 11th century. For hundreds of years, it was used as a palace, prison, and even a zoo. A steady stream of people, many of them nobles, were tortured or executed within the Tower's walls. Many visitors have reported seeing the ghosts of these unfortunate souls.

The Salt Tower is the most haunted place in the Tower of London. Even dogs will not enter here. A Yeoman Warder, one of the Tower guards, was once throttled by an unseen force in the Salt Tower. Many guards now refuse to enter after sunset.

Margaret Pole, the Countess of Salisbury, was accused of treason and sentenced to death at the Tower in 1541. Ordered to kneel for her beheading, the bold countess refused, declaring her innocence. She leapt up and ran for her life. The executioner gave chase, hacking away at the terrified woman until she finally fell dead. Over the years, on the anniversary of her grisly death, people sometimes see a spectral image of Countess Pole being chased by a ghostly axe.

Queen Anne Boleyn, the second wife of King Henry VIII, was beheaded for treason in 1536. After her execution, people claim they have seen her wandering the halls of the Tower, carrying her own head under her arm.

PHANTOM BATTLEFIELDS

O f all the places for ghosts to haunt, battlefields seem the most natural. It's said that ghosts come into existence when somebody meets a violent end. In some battles, thousands of people die in a single day. Screams of agony fill the air, and the ground is soaked with the blood of fallen soldiers. The spirits of many people who die amid such violence are unable to leave the fields of battle. They're doomed to forever wander the earth in search of their old regiments or fallen comrades. Perhaps their job is to protect the hallowed ground. Or maybe they don't realize they're dead, and they're simply trying to find a way home.

Facing Page: Search Wraith by Janny Wurts.
Below: Union and Confederate Army reenactors clash during the 139th anniversary of the Battle of Gettysburg.

Gettysburg

Gettysburg, Pennsylvania, was the site of one of the most famous battles of the American Civil War. Over a period of three days, from July 1 to July 3, 1863, Union and Confederate armies fought each other in pitched battles. The resulting carnage was breathtaking. Combined, the two sides suffered more than 46,000 casualties, of which nearly 8,000 died. It was a turning point in the war. From this time on, the Confederacy was doomed.

Immediately after the battle, the air was filled with the screams of wounded men, and the stench of blood and dead bodies.

Above: Dead soldiers lie on the Gettysburg Battlefield in July 1863. It took weeks before all the dead were buried. Many believe these soldiers still haunt the area.

Weeks passed before all the dead were buried. Hundreds of soldiers were laid to rest where they fell. Many more were collected and buried in what later would become the National Cemetery at Gettysburg.

Today, the Gettysburg Battlefield is a National Military Park. It is located in south-central Pennsylvania. Millions of people tour the site each year. Many visitors believe parts of the battlefield are haunted. They report hearing strange noises, such as muffled shouts and screams, or far-away cannons. On quiet, moonless nights, some people see glowing orbs floating over the hallowed ground. Also, lone soldiers in ragged Civil War uniforms have been spotted wandering the cemetery, as if looking for fallen comrades.

Antietam

The Battle of Antietam, also known as the Battle of Sharpsburg, took place on September 17, 1862, near Sharpsburg, Maryland. It was the single bloodiest day of the Civil War. More than 23,000 Union and Confederate soldiers fell victim to the violence. More than 3,500 were killed. Many of the casualties were taken to local houses and churches, where doctors tried to fix their wounds. Medical science was primitive by today's standards, and the soldiers suffered greatly.

One house at Grove Farm reportedly still has floorboards that are soaked in blood, which cannot be removed no matter how hard they are scrubbed.

Bloody Lane was a heavily defended Confederate position. It was a sunken country road that divided two farm fields. Union troops repeatedly attacked the Rebels, but were cut down time after time. Finally, with the help of the 69th New York Infantry (the "Irish Brigade"), the Federal troops overran the road. It quickly became a death trap for the Rebels. One Union soldier later described the action as "like shooting animals in a pen."

Today, Antietam Battlefield is preserved as a national historic site. It's said that the spirits of many dead soldiers still roam the battlefield, unable to find peace in the blood-soaked ground. Some visitors report hearing phantom gunfire that echoes down Bloody Lane, and the sound of ghostly boots can be heard marching down the gravel roads. As the sulfur smell of gunpowder drifts across the breeze, some people witness strange apparitions dressed in Union and Confederate uniforms. The visitors assume these strange visions are merely Civil War reenactors, until the soldiers suddenly vanish into the misty air.

Below: In 2002, during the 140th reenactment of the Battle of Antietam, a lone Confederate reenactor faces off against a battle line of Union infantry soldiers.

GHOSTLY HOTELS AND MOTELS

Below: The Queen Anne Hotel in San Francisco is said to be haunted by the one-time boarding school's headmistress, Mary Lake. Unlike other hotel ghosts, Mary reportedly takes care of her charges, picking up pillows and tucking blankets around sleeping guests.

They don't pay their bills, but they never leave. Hotels and motels are favorite haunts for many different spirits. From former owners to staff members to guests, all manner of spooks reside within the walls of rooming houses. Many inns actively tell their living visitors about their ghostly guests. Major cities around the world each have a list of their top ten haunted hotels. People register for rooms far in advance to have a chance to come face-to-face with a real, dead spirit. Of course, few visitors get a good night's sleep.

The Hôtel Provincial in New Orleans, Louisiana, is said to be home to a number of ghosts. The land once held a military hospital. During a séance in recent years, a military man fully materialized dressed in a khaki uniform, complete with hat and medals. He apparently lost his love, stating, "I need to leave. She doesn't love me, she loves you." His spirit haunts the hotel, and guests have reported cold chills and the eerie feeling of being watched. Footsteps, whispers, groans, and moans occur when no one is there. Staff and guests have reported opening their doors and seeing the forms of bloody soldiers lying in pain in their room. The sad spirits disappear as soon as the lights come on. Some people keep the lights on all night!

One of the most famous haunted motels didn't really exist. It was a set for Alfred Hitchcock's 1960 horror film, *Psycho*. The Bates Motel, off the main road and normally deserted, was run by Norman Bates (Anthony Perkins) and his reclusive mother. Marion Crane (Janet Leigh), a thief on the run from the law, wearily decides to spend the night. She will never leave. In a famous scene, Marion is stabbed to death in her shower. Norman discovers the body and blames his crazy mother for Marion's death. He covers up the murder, hiding the body and car in a nearby swamp. When Marion disappears, her sister Lila (Vera Miles) comes to the Bates Motel looking for answers. In a terrifying scene, she discovers Norman's grisly secret: he killed his mother years earlier and kept her body. Norman, dressed as "mother," is the killer.

Above: Maitz Motel by Don Maitz. *Below:* A poster from 1960's *Psycho*.

Restaurant Haunts

F ood and spirits are served at many restaurants. In some cases, spirits are the ghostly kind, not alcoholic drinks. Many cafes, supper clubs, pubs, and taverns have both a host and ghost on hand to take care of their hungry and thirsty customers. From fancy white-tablecloth establishments to simple neighborhood clubs, restaurants often find themselves with ghosts of former owners, chefs, and customers who just won't leave.

In New York's Greenwich Village, Chumley's restaurant and bar, a speakeasy illegally serving drinks in the 1920s, is haunted by the ghost of its one-time owner, Henrietta Chumley. She is rumored to sit near the fireplace and mischievously tip bottles off the shelves. A favorite hangout for firefighters, the current owners sadly learned several of their customers were killed on September 11, 2001, when two airliners were flown into the World Trade Center in Manhattan. Reportedly, those firefighters return to their favorite haunt to play the jukebox, even when it's unplugged.

The Boot and Slipper in Amersham, England, has a resident ghost who mutters to itself, pushes past staff and customers, and puts a less-than comforting hand on people's shoulders. Stay out of the 15th-century pub's cellar—the ghost appears there regularly.

Facing Page: Haunted Hops by Don Maitz. *Below:* Chumley's restaurant and bar is home to a number of ghosts, including its former owner.

EERIE LIGHTHOUSES

A lightkeeper's life was often an isolated and lonely one. Lighthouses were built on distant, towering locations. Keepers had only limited opportunities to go to the nearest town. During the winter, some found themselves trapped for months on the small piece of rock and ground that was their home. Even if a keeper's family joined him at the lighthouse, he worked during the night, while they slept, and slept while they were awake. For some, it was a way of life that they loved. Others were driven insane.

The 30-foot (9-m) Owl's Head Lighthouse in Owl's Head, Maine, is unusually short by lighthouse standards. But it is long on haunted history. In fact, the squat, black-and-white brick tower and keeper's house has been named the number one haunted lighthouse in America.

Built in 1852 to watch over Rockland Harbor and Penobscot Bay, the Owl's Head Light remains in use as a Coast Guard residence. Reports of spirit activity include an old keeper who doesn't want to leave. Apparently he is very frugal, as he keeps turning down the heat. His footprints have been seen in the tower and surrounding area, and some people have heard his heavy steps. He sometimes appears to be polishing the light's brass fixtures, but mysteriously disappears when someone turns to look at him. In addition, an older woman known as "Little Lady" also resides at Owl's Head Light. Often seen in the residence's kitchen, people report feeling comforted, not frightened, when she appears.

Members of the Coast Guard, the current residents of Owl's Head Light, also report a spirit who jumps into bed with them. Denise Germann said she once rolled over, thinking her husband was climbing into bed. Instead, she saw "the indentation of a body lying next to me. This form was… moving." She wasn't afraid of the visitor, but did ask him to stop moving around so she could sleep. Was it a dream? Germann doesn't think so.

Facing Page:
Shipwrecker by Janny Wurts.
Below: An antique postcard of Owl's Head Lighthouse.

Above: A lonely lighthouse shrouded in dark clouds. Many lighthouse keepers claim they share their nightly duties with ghosts.

Battery Point Lighthouse protects the area surrounding Crescent City, California. The unique lighthouse is only accessible during low tide. The rest of the time, it sits as an island beacon—which happens to be haunted.

Built in 1856, the lighthouse is connected to the mainland by a 200-foot (61-m) tongue of rock and land. As long as the ocean remains relatively calm, people may walk across the isthmus between 10:00 am and 4:00 pm. But visitors must pay attention to the time. Once the water starts to rise, people may find themselves trapped on the island with a ghostly spirit who enjoys the near-solitude that each night brings.

The fun-loving ghost has been known to visit the lighthouse's attached home, sending a rocking chair in motion, causing a disconnected old telephone to ring, and mischievously moving the caretaker's slippers.

Who is this ghost? No one knows, although some people report the vague smell of pipe tobacco and footsteps on the stairs when no one is nearby. But there are also stories of a woman singing. Could there be more than one ghost in the stone-and-brick lighthouse? Whether there's one spirit or more, the lighthouse keeper's cat is quick to leave when the ghost's presence is felt.

Above: The moon descends eerily behind the Ludington Lighthouse in Michigan. Many lighthouses are reported to be haunted by former keepers who have stayed at their posts.

GLOSSARY

APPARITION
A sudden, startling supernatural appearance of a person or thing, such as a ghost, that appears real.

CELTIC
Refers to the people or language of the Celts, who dominated the British Isles and parts of France and Scandinavia for hundreds of years before the Roman invasion and occupation of 43 A.D.

EXORCISE
The attempt, usually by a priest or other religious figure, to force an evil spirit to leave a particular place or person.

ISTHMUS
A narrow strip of land, with water on either side, which acts as a connector between two land forms.

MIDDLE AGES
In European history, a period defined by historians as between 476 A.D. and 1450 A.D.

NOBLE
Someone born into a class of people who have high social or political status. Sometimes ordinary people could be made nobles by doing something extraordinary, like fighting well on the battlefield. Usually, however, only people who are the sons or daughters of nobles get to be nobles themselves.

PARANORMAL
An experience or perception that is supernatural, which cannot be explained by science.

PHANTOM
Something that does not actually exist but seems apparent to the senses. A phantom may be the result of a mirage or optical illusion.

Above: Desperation: The Well by Don Maitz.

POLTERGEIST
Ghosts who make noise and like to make their presence known. "Poltergeist" comes from the German words for "knock" and "spirit."

PSYCHIC
A person with extraordinary perception and understanding of the human mind. A psychic is especially sensitive to supernatural forces and influences.

SPECTER
Something apparently seen that is not in the physical world, especially a scary vision.

INDEX